DEADLY WEAPONS

A Play

by

LAURIE BROOKS

Dramatic Publishing
Woodstock, Illinois • England • Australia • New Zealand

for my sister
Emelie FitzGibbon,
with love and gratitude

* * * *

The author would like to gratefully acknowledge and thank the following for their nurturing and support of this play: Emelie FitzGibbon and Graffiti Theatre Company, Graham Whitehead, Lowell Swortzell and the New York University Program in Educational Theatre's New Plays for Young Audiences at the Provincetown Playhouse, Robyn Flatt and the Dallas Children's Theater Young Adult Series, Jeff Church and, for ongoing inspiration, my three daughters, Joanna, Liz and Stephanie.

Deadly Weapons is listed in ASSITEJ/USA Outstanding Plays for Young Audiences, Vol. VI, 1999.

IMPORTANT BILLING AND CREDIT REQUIREMENTS

All producers of the play *must* give credit to the author(s) of the play in all programs distributed in connection with performances of the play and in all instances in which the title of the play appears for purposes of advertising, publicizing or otherwise exploiting the play and/or a production. The name of the author(s) *must* also appear on a separate line, on which no other name appears, immediately following the title, and *must* appear in size of type not less than fifty percent the size of the title type. Biographical information on the author(s), if included in this book, may be used on all programs. *On all programs this notice must appear:*

"Produced by special arrangement with
THE DRAMATIC PUBLISHING COMPANY of Woodstock, Illinois"

Introduction

Suddenly, there were three characters in the room. Demanding, secretive, vulnerable, they compelled our attention, taking us on a dark adventure into uncomfortable places. We followed.

This was the extraordinary and seminal moment in the devising room that saw the genesis of *Deadly Weapons*. Laurie Brooks had come to Ireland to work with Graffiti Theatre Company on a new script. *Deadly Weapons* was the result, an ideal mix of educationally provocative ideas embedded in a fast-paced thriller aimed at fourteen- to sixteen-year-olds. The play became our 1998 fall tour, a successful and challenging experience for both students and teachers who found themselves deeply invested in the recognisable young characters in the play.

Serena is new to the neighbourhood, desperate to belong to the seemingly more glamorous world of Moss and Jessie. Challenged by them, she accepts a dare to do something deadly dangerous. However, a secret that Serena keeps will turn the dare into a nightmare and force these three young adults to confront the nature of their relationships and their responsibilities to themselves and each other. The "deadly weapons" of Laurie Brooks' play are more than the literal ones on the charge sheet, they are sharply embedded in family, society, peer relations—in ourselves.

Deadly Weapons is a play about vulnerability, about hurt and about challenges. It speaks to young adults and those who work with and for them. Its voices are real voices. As one thirteen-year-old audience member said to me, "I know these people." It is this recognition which makes the play compelling. Everyone in the audience empathizes with at least one of the characters and identifies with the landslide from a deceptively simple dare to "be one of us," into a relentless spiral of damaging consequences.

With simple staging requirements and a cast of four, *Deadly Weapons* is immensely flexible for touring production. It is, moreover, an exciting play to direct in its demand to achieve both the relentless forward momentum of the plot and the subtle nuances required of the actors.

Deadly Weapons is theatre which treats a young adult audience with respect and recognition; portraying the toughness and absolutism of both their world and their mind-sets while respecting their ability to identify and analyze the anti-models presented. It is an edgy play, one at the current boundaries of the genre. But it is a play that enables us to hear the energized and engaged response of the young audience and feel their frisson of recognition.

As the audience of *Deadly Weapons*, we are challenged by competing sympathies underlying a tense and driven plot. As directors, actors and explorers we are challenged to investigate and inhabit the vital reality of this charged and dangerous world.

Emelie FitzGibbon, Artistic Director,
Graffiti Theatre Company,
Cork, Ireland

Deadly Weapons was commissioned, devised with and premiered by Graffiti Theatre Company, Cork, Ireland, September 21, 1998.

Mossie . . . . DAVID KELLY
Jess . . . . NORA MULLIN
Sinead . . . . ANNA PLATT
Conroy . . . . JOHN LOVETT

Director . . . . EMELIE FITZGIBBON
Fight Director . . . . CHARLIE RUXTON
Set Design . . . . KURT BIPPERT
Production Manager . . . . NIGEL VUKASINOVIC
Sound Production . . . . ROGER GREGG
Education Officer . . . . SEONA NI BHRIAIN
Devising Company . . . . DAVID KELLY, KURT BIPPERT,
DIANE O'KEEFFE, EVEANNA O'MEARA,
SEONA NI BHRIAIN, BRYAN HARTEN

Deadly Weapons was presented in a rehearsed reading at New York University Program in Educational Theatre's New Plays for Young Audiences at the Provincetown Playhouse, New York City, June 23, 24 and 25, 2000.

Moss . . . . SHANNON GANNON, DENNIS WALTER
Jessie . . . . JANE WILSON
Serena . . . . JENNIFER SMOLOS
Conroy . . . . WILL BARTLETT
Stage Directions . . . . . DENNIS WALTER, SHANNON GANNON

Director . . . . GRAHAM WHITEHEAD
Stage Manager . . . . MICHELLE BERTI
Designer . . . . JASON LIVINGSTON
Producer . . . . MELISSA SWICK
Program Director . . . . LOWELL SWORTZELL

Deadly Weapons was presented at a Dark Night Staged Reading at Dallas Children's Theater with the support of Presbyterian Health Care, November 2000.

Moss .... DERIK WEBB
Jessie .... STEPHANIE YBARRA
Serena........................... KATE BLACKSTONE
Old Man Leisner .... PAT KELLEY
Stage Directions........................ KELLY ABBOTT

Director .... GRAHAM WHITEHEAD

The American premiere of *Deadly Weapons* was the inaugural play in Dallas Children's Theater's Young Adult Series at the Crescent Theater, March 1, 2002.

Moss.................................... DERIK WEBB
Jessie .... STEPHANIE YBARRA
Serena........................... KATE BLACKSTONE
Old Man Leisner.................. TERRY VANDIVORT

Director .... GRAHAM WHITEHEAD
Set Design .... MARY THERESE D'AVIGNON
Lighting Design .... LINDA BLASE
Sound Design....................... MARCO E. SALINAS
Costume Design........................ DIANE SIMONS
Prop Design .... HEATHER WILLINGHAM
Executive Artistic Director .... ROBYN FLATT
Associate Artistic Director................ ARTIE OLAISEN

DEADLY WEAPONS

A Play in One Act
For 2 Men and 2 Women

CHARACTERS

JESSIE. . . . . female, 15 years old

MOSS . . . . male, 15 years old

SERENA . . . . female, 15 years old

OLD MAN LEISNER . . . . in his 40s

SETTING: Serena's house and Leisner's loft.

TIME: The present.

DEADLY WEAPONS

(In the blackout, loud metal sound effects or heavy metal music. Enter JESSIE, MOSS and SERENA, shining flashlights over the audience. Sound effects climax and fade but remain under the monologues. SERENA and JESSIE focus their flashlights on MOSS as he speaks.)

MOSS. It's no big deal. I expect Brian to beat the shit out of me. It's not so bad. He goes on at me for a while then it's over. He says get out of my sight. You make me sick. You're the one who's sick, I think, but I don't say nothin'. Brian's cool. Nobody gets in his way. Sometimes he lets me run errands for him, 'cause I'm his brother. Not the big stuff, 'cause I screw up sometimes, but Brian says I'll learn, if he doesn't kill me first. I hang out with Jessie mostly. Jessie and me are just waiting. Waiting for our chance to do somethin'. Somethin' big. Then Brian'll treat us different. He'll show us respect. And if Brian respects us, everyone will.

(Sound effects surge and fade. MOSS and SERENA turn their flashlights on JESSIE.)

JESSIE. Every day I got to deal with her. Her eyes all glazed over and empty, like there's nothing there. This morning, one piece of hair was stickin' up right out of the top of her head like she'd been sleepin' on it too long and it grew that way. She looked funny as hell, but somehow I couldn't bring myself to laugh. She was too pathetic. Her with her Bible study group. She's always tryin' to get me to go to church with her! She can't make me go. Not anymore. She says I'll go to hell, but I don't care. She whines and moans and talks about the devil. She never gives up. Soon I'll be out of there and I won't have to deal with her stupid rules and the pathetic way she looks at me. She doesn't have a clue who I really am. Nobody does. Not yet.

(Sound effects surge and fade. MOSS and JESSIE turn their flashlights on SERENA.)

SERENA. I think a lot about what it would be like to be in the movies. You could be a different person, someone brave and beautiful and extraordinary. And with each movie you'd have the chance to be someone new. That's what I'd like, to be someone new. I never told anybody that. They'd probably just laugh. I know Jessie would. She laughs at everything. But she's cool. And she's tough. Not like me. Mom says that things change. Every day's another chance and that hard times make us stronger. I think she's right about the hard times part. But when I told her that, you know what she did? She started cryin'. You'd think she would have been happy to hear how she was right about somethin'.

(Sound effects surge. All three characters swing their flashlights over the audience. Sound effects fade.)

(Lights shift. SERENA's house. MOSS sprawls. SERENA looks out the window. JESSIE does SERENA's hair.)

JESSIE. Pull it off your face like this, Serena. See? It shows off your eyes.

SERENA. You think so? I usually wear it down.

JESSIE. This is much better. It doesn't hide your face. You like it, Moss?

MOSS. It's awright.

JESSIE. What do you know. It looks great. You should wear it like that all the time.

SERENA. Thanks, Jessie. I mean for showin' me around and all.

JESSIE. Hey, I know what it's like to be new. When my dad was around he used to drag us all over the place. We moved four times one year. You just stick with me and Moss. We'll take care of you.

MOSS. Yeah, we'll be like your bodyguards.

JESSIE. I wish there was somethin' to do. This day is so boring. My whole life is utterly, completely boring.

MOSS. Shut up. You're makin' it worse. Whinin' about it.

JESSIE. I can complain if I feel like it.

MOSS. Then go somewhere else so I don't have to hear it.

JESSIE *(yelling in his face)*. Bored. I'm bored. I'm so bored I could die.

MOSS. Get off me.

SERENA. Let's go somewhere.

JESSIE. Where?

SERENA. I dunno. Anywhere but here. There's nothin' to do here.

MOSS. We could watch TV.

SERENA. I'm sick of TV.

MOSS. That's because you got one in your room. If I had a TV in my room, I'd lock the door and channel surf all day with no one getting in my way.

SERENA. Sssshhhh.

JESSIE. What?

SERENA. I thought I heard my dad. He'll be home any minute.

JESSIE. So what?

SERENA. So nothin'.

JESSIE. So she's not allowed to hang out with us. Daddy's princess.

SERENA. That's not it. I just don't like it here. Let's go somewhere else.

MOSS. Where?

SERENA. Dunno. Somewhere. Somewhere deadly fun.

JESSIE. That's nowhere.

MOSS. We could go to the movies.

JESSIE (making fun of him). "We could go to the movies."

MOSS. What's wrong with that? Brian might be there.

JESSIE. Will you stop yappin' about Brian? I don't want to see Brian and neither does Serena. Do you, Serena?

SERENA. No.

JESSIE. What's your problem? Why are you staring at her?

MOSS. I'm not staring at her. I'm just lookin' over there, awright?

JESSIE. Sure, Moss.

MOSS. I'm goin' to find Brian.

JESSIE. Not me. I'm done with Brian.

MOSS. That again. It wasn't Brian's fault.

JESSIE. Oh, no? Who grabbed the bag?

MOSS. It wasn't his fault he got caught.

JESSIE. Who's fault was it I spent the night at the police station?

MOSS. He didn't mean for that to happen.

JESSIE. Sure he didn't. That's why he told them I took the money.

MOSS. He never said that.

JESSIE. It took me all night to talk my way out of it. So much for trust. You'd think I'd learn.

MOSS. Brian'll make it up to you. He never forgets a favor.

JESSIE. I'm countin' on that. Serena, can I wear your bracelet again?

SERENA. This one?

JESSIE. Yeah. I love that. It's deadly.

SERENA. Here. (*She takes off the bracelet and puts it on JESSIE.*) Looks good on you.

JESSIE. Yeah. I love those smoky beads.

SERENA. You can keep it if you want to.

JESSIE. Really? Keep it?

SERENA. It looks better on you anyway.

JESSIE. You think so?

SERENA. Yeah.

JESSIE. It's like a present, right?

SERENA. Yeah.

JESSIE. Thanks. (*Pause.*) Guess you got plenty more where that came from. Hey, Moss... you got any smokes?

MOSS. Brian took 'em.

JESSIE. Got any money?

MOSS (*digging in his pockets*). Two dollars.

JESSIE. Two dollars!

(*JESSIE and SERENA laugh.*)

MOSS. Shut up. I can't help it if that's all I have.

JESSIE. Wait. Where's the money your mom gave you for those school books?

MOSS. Forget that. Let's do something deadly fun.

JESSIE. Come on. We could use that money. Thirty dollars, wasn't it?

MOSS. It's for books.

JESSIE. So what? Give it here.

MOSS. Get away.

JESSIE. I only want some of it. Come on.

MOSS. I don't have it.

JESSIE. Let's go get it then.

MOSS. I said no.

JESSIE. You don't have it, do you?

MOSS. I wouldn't give it to you anyway.

JESSIE. Aawwww, did big brother Brian take it from his little brother? Bullied it out of you, I bet. Poor Mossie. Only got two dollars.

MOSS. Brian didn't take it. I gave it to him.

JESSIE. You gave it to him? What for?

MOSS. He needed it, awright?

JESSIE. Liar. He took it from you. He always does.

MOSS. Shut up. Besides, what've you got?

JESSIE. I'd rather have nothin' than brag about two dollars. Dumbass. How about Daddy's princess? Serena's got money.

SERENA. Spent it all on CDs.

MOSS. It's not fair. You got a TV in your room, too.

JESSIE. You got it all, Serena. Daddy's big bucks, this incredible place and every teacher in school in your hip pocket. Miss Honors class up her ass.

SERENA. I can't help it if that's where they put me. I hate it.

JESSIE. But you can get money, can't you?

SERENA. My mom took her purse with her.

(MOSS takes out a knife and begins playing with it.)

JESSIE. So freakin' boring.

MOSS. Nothin' ever happens around here.

JESSIE. Put that knife away. You'll hurt yourself.

MOSS. I can play with my own knife, can't I?

JESSIE. Hey. Let me see that.

MOSS. No. Get outa here.

JESSIE. That's Brian's knife.

MOSS. No, it's not. It's mine.

JESSIE. That's Brian's switchblade. I recognize it. It's got little skeletons on it.

MOSS. It's mine now.

JESSIE. You used your old lady's money to buy Brian's knife? No. Brian loves that knife. He wouldn't sell it to you for a hundred dollars.

MOSS. That's right.

JESSIE. Then how did you get it?

MOSS. Took it. Last night while he was sleepin' like a baby.

JESSIE. You're crazy. He'll kill you when he finds out.

MOSS. He took my book money. Said he needed it. Well, I need this knife. For protection.

JESSIE. You'll need it for protection all right when Brian finds out you took it.

MOSS. He won't find out.

JESSIE. He will if somebody tells him.

MOSS. But nobody will. If they want to keep breathing.

JESSIE. I'm not afraid of you. Tough boy.

MOSS (*playing with the knife*). Maybe you should be.

JESSIE. Serena?

SERENA. What?

JESSIE. Moss likes you.

MOSS. Shut up.

JESSIE. He's got it bad for you.

MOSS. Shut up. Don't listen to her. She's lookin' for trouble.

JESSIE. It's true. He's been drooling over you since you showed up.

MOSS. Liar.

JESSIE. Just thought Serena oughta know.

MOSS. She's not listenin' to you.

SERENA. Stop it, both of you. Let's do something.

MOSS. If you tell about the knife, I'll tell Brian about you.

JESSIE. He wouldn't believe anything you told him.

MOSS. Shut up about the knife and I won't tell about... well, you know.

JESSIE. If you tell Brian anything about that you'll wish you were dead.

SERENA. Hey. I got these.

JESSIE. What you got?

MOSS. Lemme see.

JESSIE. Yeah. Let's see...

SERENA. Promise you won't laugh.

MOSS (*putting away the knife*). It's stupid. I can tell already.

JESSIE. Shut up, Moss. What you got, Serena?

SERENA. I've got three of these. Fortunetelling fish.

MOSS. What?

JESSIE. Fortunetelling fish.

MOSS. Told you it was stupid.

JESSIE. You're the one who's stupid.

SERENA. You hold it in your hand and it tells your fortune by how it moves. There's a chart that tells you the meanings.

JESSIE. Cool. Moss, you go.

MOSS. I'm not goin'.

JESSIE. Let's hear your fortune. This oughta be good.

MOSS. Not me.

JESSIE. You chicken? *(She teases MOSS with chicken sounds.)*

MOSS. I'm not chicken, you are. You go first.

JESSIE. If you're not chicken, then why won't you go first?

MOSS. I always have to go first.

SERENA. I'll go first. Jessie, you don't think it's stupid, do you?

MOSS. I think it's stupid.

JESSIE. You're stupid. Let's see, Serena. *(JESSIE takes the cellophane fish out of its wrapper and places it in the palm of her hand which she holds out in front of her.)* Its tail. It's moving! Look!

SERENA. It's all wavy.

MOSS. Jeeze!

JESSIE. What does it mean?

SERENA. Here. Look it up. *(SERENA gives the wrapper to MOSS. JESSIE snatches the wrapper.)*

JESSIE. Don't give it to him. Give it here.

SERENA. It's still moving. What does it say?

JESSIE. Moving tail. Independence.

MOSS. What?

JESSIE. Independence, dumbass!

MOSS. What's that mean?

JESSIE. It means on your own, stupid.

MOSS. I know that. I mean what's the fortune?

SERENA. We have to figure it out. Wait and see what happens.

MOSS. That's stupid.

JESSIE. Ignore him, Serena. Independence is a great fortune. Maybe it means you'll be out on your own before you know it.

SERENA. I'd give anything to be on my own. Away from home.

JESSIE. Yeah. That'd be great.

SERENA. I hate it here. I hate it so much. I wish I was dead.

(JESSIE and MOSS exchange an uncomfortable look.)

JESSIE. Hey. You don't mean that, Princess.

SERENA. Can we go to your house, Jessie?

JESSIE. I hate my house. Ma's always home. Breathin' down my back. Talkin' some religious shit.

SERENA *(looking out the window)*. Yeah. My dad's always on my case. He inspects my homework every night.

MOSS. Why?

JESSIE. Because she's Daddy's princess, that's why.

SERENA. He's gonna be home soon. I know it.

JESSIE. Then we'll leave. But I like it here, don't you, Moss?

MOSS. Yeah. It's clean. Shiny.

JESSIE. And no one to bother us.

SERENA. Yeah. I can do whatever I want. My parents just don't like people over is all.

JESSIE. Especially people like us.

MOSS. Here. Give me a fish.

SERENA. I don't know if I should. You said it was stupid. Twice.

MOSS. I didn't mean it. You know I didn't.

JESSIE. Aw, give him one. Big baby.

(SERENA gives him a fish.)

MOSS. What do I do?

SERENA. Just take it out of the package and hold it in your hand. Like this.

MOSS. That tickles.

SERENA. Hold still.

JESSIE. It's not moving.

MOSS *(to the fish)*. Come on, you, move.

SERENA. Just wait.

MOSS. Move, you jerk! I was right. This is stupid.

JESSIE. Here. I'll try mine. *(She takes the fish out of the wrapper and places it in her hand.)* Now we'll see who gets the good fortune.

SERENA *(laughing)*. Fickle! That's what yours is. See how it's curling up on the sides.

JESSIE. Here. Let me see that.

SERENA. Look. It's turning over. What's that mean?

JESSIE. Turns over ... never mind. This is stupid.

MOSS. Let me see that. *(He grabs the paper out of JESSIE's hand. Reads with difficulty.)* "Turns over ... *(Pause.)* ... false." That's what it says here ... false.

JESSIE. I ain't false. I'm all real—every little part of me.

SERENA. Not that kind of false. Like untrue.

JESSIE. I ain't that kind of false either.

MOSS. Even that stupid fish knows what a liar you are.

SERENA. It's not supposed to be serious. It's just for laughs, that's all.

JESSIE. It's not funny.

MOSS. Hey. Mine's still lyin' there. It's not movin'.

SERENA. It's a dead one.

MOSS. What?

SERENA. That's your fortune. Dead one.

MOSS. Who me? I'm a dead one?

(The girls laugh riotously.)

JESSIE. That's you, all right, a dead one ... when Brian finds out about the knife.

MOSS. Shut up.

JESSIE. Make me.

(MOSS goes to grab JESSIE. SERENA cowers and cries out.)

SERENA. Stop it!

JESSIE. What's the matter with you? If he really laid a finger on me, I'd kick his ass.

MOSS. I'm not gonna beat up a girl. *(He gets JESSIE in a playful headlock.)*

SERENA. Stop it!

JESSIE *(grabbing MOSS by the front of his shirt)*. Try it and see what happens.

MOSS. You can't bully me. I'm bigger'n you.

JESSIE. You may be bigger but I'm tougher.

SERENA. Stop it! You're no fun.

JESSIE. What do you mean, we did your stupid fish, didn't we? You're the only one who got a half-decent fortune, Princess Independence.

SERENA. That's not my fault.

(Silence. MOSS takes out the knife again.)

JESSIE. It's so boring I could scream. *(She screams, then covers her mouth and giggles.)*

SERENA. Sssshhhh!

JESSIE. I know. We're not supposed to be here. Miss AP class isn't supposed to be seen with losers like us. *(She playfully pushes SERENA's back. SERENA overreacts, wincing and pulling away.)*

SERENA. Don't do that.

JESSIE. Do what, I hardly touched you.

SERENA. Well don't, okay?

JESSIE. Oooo, sensitive. You'd think I punched you or something. Wouldn't want to hurt Her Royal Highness.

MOSS. Why do you have to be such a bitch?

JESSIE. Just comes natural, I guess. *(Pause.)* I wish someone'd get murdered.

MOSS. That'd be deadly. Hey, here's who oughta get killed.

(MOSS imitates OLD MAN LEISNER—strange walk, dropping tools, odd expression. JESSIE and SERENA laugh. MOSS ambles up to them and squints in their faces.)

MOSS. "Have you...

ALL *(yelling)*. ...seen my Corky?"

JESSIE. Old Man Leisner! *(They laugh.)* Disgusting.

SERENA. He's so creepy.

MOSS. He almost got killed again yesterday, out lookin' for Corky.

JESSIE. Go on. Tell.

MOSS. He's walkin' up the street. All his tools strapped on, making an awful racket, like a freakin' one-man parade. He's crossin' the street, not lookin' where he's goin'. All of a sudden a car comes around the corner and I think he's dead meat.

SERENA. Oh, my God!

MOSS. But the car swerves at the last minute and misses him by this much. Another second and that would have been it. Dead. So there he is lyin' in the street. All his stuff strewn around like garbage. He starts yellin'! You know how he does. *(Imitating.)* "Corky! Corky!"

SERENA. Did you help him?

MOSS. Help him? I wouldn't go near that weirdo. He's crawlin' toward me, so I get away as quick as I can.

JESSIE. Why didn't you just cross the street? You knew he was gonna say it.

MOSS *(imitating LEISNER)*. "Have you seen my Corky?"

(They laugh.)

SERENA. It's creepy. The way he says that since Corky's gone.

JESSIE. You'd think he'd be relieved to be rid of him.

MOSS. Yeah. Corky's a real jerk. Just like his old man. Always tryin' to tag along with Brian. Couldn't take a hint. Remember that time they took him outside of town, left him in the road and drove off?

JESSIE. That was deadly. He totally lost it.

MOSS. It was awesome. I never saw anybody so mad. Punchin' the air and throwin' rocks and stuff.

JESSIE. He finally got the message.

MOSS. For a while.

JESSIE. Until that guy called Brian a fag and Corky kicked the crap out of him. Now he's Brian's shadow.

MOSS. I'm Brian's shadow.

JESSIE. What a loser.

MOSS. Shut up.

JESSIE. What? I was talkin' about Corky.

SERENA. You shouldn't speak ill of the dead.

MOSS. We don't know if he's dead. He's just missing's all.

JESSIE. I heard the old man killed Corky.

SERENA. True enough. I heard it, too.

JESSIE. Locked him in the basement and starved him to death. That's what I heard.

SERENA. That's disgusting.

MOSS. Corky's such a jerk. I shoulda killed him.

JESSIE. Stop tryin' to be like Brian. You couldn't kill anybody.

MOSS. I was just saying he was a real weirdo. Just like his old man.

SERENA. You think he's dead?

JESSIE. Yeah. I think he's dead.

MOSS. The cops think he's dead. They spent two days questioning Old Man Leisner.

JESSIE. I think Old Man Leisner killed Corky and the body's still in the house.

MOSS. Must stink somethin' awful!

JESSIE. Like shit warmed over!

SERENA. How come the police didn't find the body if it's still in there?

JESSIE. Maybe Old Man Leisner convinced the cops he didn't kill Corky. But we know different, huh, Moss?

MOSS. Yeah. We know better than the cops what goes on around here. And anything we don't know, Brian knows.

JESSIE. If it's bad, Brian knows.

SERENA. I'm scared of Brian.

JESSIE. Everyone's scared of Brian. If they're smart.

MOSS. I ain't scared of my own brother.

JESSIE. I rest my case.

SERENA. Old Man Leisner did some work at my house when we moved in. Ma said he could paint the fence.

JESSIE. God. How could you stand having him around?

MOSS. The way he's always twitchin' and talking to himself.

JESSIE. Or yelling at somebody.

SERENA. He didn't say anything the whole time he was there. Just painted.

MOSS. And acted weird.

SERENA. I felt sorry for him.

JESSIE. You would. You're lucky he didn't murder you.

SERENA. Corky showed up outside the house one day. They got into an awful fight. Yelling and screaming.

JESSIE. What happened?

SERENA. I don't know. I was up in my room. I heard their voices. But there must have been a fight because there was a kind of crashing like someone fell down. Dad went out and told them to go home and don't come back. He finished the fence himself.

MOSS. I hate that old pervert. I hate Corky, too. But his old man's worse. Everyone knows he's crazy.

SERENA. There was paint all over where they had the fight.

JESSIE. Jesus. I'm glad he's not my old man.

MOSS. You don't have an old man.

JESSIE. Shut up. I'd rather have no old man than him, all right?

MOSS. You don't have to shout.

SERENA. He shouldn't have hurt his own son.

JESSIE. He didn't hurt him. He murdered him in cold blood.

MOSS. And he wasn't even punished. Got clean away with it.

SERENA. Somebody should do something about it.

(The three think on this.)

MOSS. Somebody should steal his precious tools.

JESSIE. Yeah, or smash up his place.

MOSS. That'd teach him.

JESSIE. Yeah.

MOSS. I dare you.

JESSIE. What?

MOSS. I dare you to go into that house.

JESSIE. What? Leisner's place? You're crazy.

MOSS. Now who's chicken. *(He makes chicken sounds.)*

JESSIE. Shut up. I'm not chicken. I'll go if you'll go.

MOSS. I'll go.

JESSIE. He won't even be home. He goes out drinkin' every night.

MOSS. Yeah, I seen him goin' into the Candlelight.

JESSIE. Probably chuggin' a few with your old man!

MOSS. Shut up about my old man.

JESSIE. What? You're always saying about him being drunk every night.

MOSS. Don't you talk about him, awright?

JESSIE. So it's only you can talk about him, huh?

MOSS. That's right. So shut up.

JESSIE. God. You'd think I bad-mouthed the pope. No, Brian!

(JESSIE and SERENA laugh. MOSS looks stricken.)

SERENA. You didn't mean anything, did you, Jessie?

JESSIE. I didn't mean anything, you big baby.

MOSS. Let's go. We'll slip into the house, check it out, and no one'll know we were ever even in the place. Maybe we can prove he killed Corky. Deadly!

JESSIE. Like detectives. What a gas!

MOSS. What do you say, Serena?

SERENA. Don't know.

JESSIE. What? It was your idea.

SERENA. It was not.

MOSS. You said somebody should do something.

SERENA. I didn't mean us.

JESSIE. Oh, Daddy's princess. Afraid her mom and dad'll find out she's not perfect. But you're one of us, aren't you, Serena. Deep down. Well, almost. You just never been initiated, right, Moss?

MOSS. Huh? That's right. She hasn't been initiated.

JESSIE. This is the perfect chance.

SERENA. What do I have to do?

JESSIE. Nothin'. You'll go in the house with us. That's all.

SERENA. I can't.

JESSIE. Why not?

SERENA. Because it's against the law.

MOSS. Well, I couldn't do anything against the law, could you?

JESSIE. Not me. I'd rather die first. Come off it, Serena.

SERENA. What if we get caught?

MOSS. We won't get caught.

SERENA. But what if we do?

JESSIE. We'll blame it on you. Tell 'em it was all your idea.

(JESSIE and MOSS find this hilarious.)

SERENA. Forget it. I'm not going.

JESSIE. Serena. It was a joke. We're in this together. We won't get caught. It'll be amazing.

SERENA. I can't go. I'll stay here.

JESSIE. Okay, Daddy's princess.

SERENA. I'm not anybody's princess.

JESSIE. That's up to you. Do you want to be one of us?

SERENA. You know I do.

JESSIE. It'll be an adventure. And since we can't tell anyone, we'll be bound together with a secret.

MOSS. Unless we find the body.

JESSIE. Yeah. That'd be deadly. We'd be heroes.

MOSS. Maybe there's a reward.

SERENA. Maybe our pictures'd be in the paper. TRIO OF TEENS RIGHTS A WRONG!

MOSS. Deadly!

SERENA. No, it just doesn't seem fair somehow.

JESSIE. Fair? Fair to who? Old Man Leisner?

(JESSIE and MOSS laugh.)

MOSS. Was he fair to Corky?

JESSIE. Nothin's fair. Is it fair the cops kept me in jail overnight for snatching that bag when it was Brian who took it? Is it fair they let Old Man Leisner get away with killing his son? Is it fair my old man ran off and left us? Is that fair? It's us got to make what's fair.

SERENA. I don't know.

JESSIE. "I don't know" isn't good enough. Either you're in or you're out. You've got to be initiated. You've got to earn your place.

MOSS. She doesn't want to go, Jess. She's out.

JESSIE. She's in. And she'll go in first. Right, Serena? Right?

MOSS. Leave her alone, Jess.

JESSIE. I said she'll go in first.

SERENA. Yes. All right.

MOSS. And I'll bring my knife. For protection.

JESSIE. You're crazy. We won't need Brian's stupid knife.

MOSS. It's my knife now.

SERENA. I've got candles.

JESSIE. Deadly. I love candles.

MOSS. Candles are stupid.

JESSIE. Flashlights. You got any flashlights?

SERENA. Lots. My dad's always using them for some job or other.

JESSIE. Cool.

MOSS. Let's go.

SERENA. Wait. We have to swear.

MOSS. Swear what?

SERENA. An oath.

JESSIE. What kind of oath?

SERENA. A sacred oath that binds us together.

MOSS. That's stupid.

JESSIE. I like it. If she's goin' to be initiated, we swear a sacred oath.

SERENA. Yeah.

MOSS. I'm not swearin' a stupid oath.

JESSIE. Then you're not going.

MOSS. That's not fair.

JESSIE. Yes, it is. If you won't swear, then how can we trust you?

MOSS. I wouldn't trust you if you swore on a stack of Bibles.

JESSIE. You have to swear or you can't go.

MOSS. What makes you think you're in charge here?

JESSIE. Because I am.

MOSS. All right. But it's stupid.

SERENA. Take hands.

JESSIE. I got your back. You can trust me. And even if we get caught, I'll never tell.

SERENA. I swear.

JESSIE. I swear. *(Pause.)* Moss?

MOSS. I swear, awright?

JESSIE. Now it's our secret forever.

SERENA. Forever and ever.

(Blackout. Exit SERENA, MOSS and JESSIE. Sound effects as before.)

(Lights shift. Night. Leisner's squalid loft. Clanking, banging sound of the three trying to get the skylight open. The space is in darkness except for light from the street coming in the windows. SERENA crawls in through the skylight, followed by JESSIE.)

MOSS (*offstage*). Hurry! I hear someone coming.

JESSIE. I'm goin' as fast as I can.

SERENA. Here. I'll catch you.

JESSIE. God. It's a long way down.

SERENA. I'll catch you.

MOSS. Sssshhh. Shut up.

(*The sound of footsteps approaching, then receding. JESSIE more or less falls through the open window onto the floor.*)

JESSIE. Come on, Moss.

MOSS. I'm comin'. I'm comin'. Jesus, I can't fit through. Aaahhh.

SERENA. Shhh. You're makin' too much noise.

MOSS. Who cares? There's no one to hear us.

JESSIE (*shouting*). No one in the world.

(*MOSS drops through the skylight to the floor.*)

JESSIE. God. It's dark in here. I can't see my hands in front of my face. (*SERENA turns on her flashlight.*) That's better. (*JESSIE turns on her flashlight.*)

MOSS. I need a flashlight.

JESSIE. There's only two so shut up about it.

MOSS. It's not fair that I don't get one.

JESSIE. Will you stop whining. Let's check it out.

(*MOSS retreats into the shadows.*)

SERENA. This place is a mess.

JESSIE. What a pigsty. (*She moves around the space.*)

SERENA. Be careful.

JESSIE *(bumping her leg)*. What's that. I hurt myself. *(She shines her flashlight on it.)* It's a stupid hacksaw.

MOSS. Is there blood on it? Maybe Old Man Leisner used it to hack up the body and hide the parts.

SERENA. He couldn't have.

MOSS. Sure he could. Then if the cops came snoopin' around, they wouldn't find the body.

SERENA. That's disgusting.

JESSIE *(shining her flashlight around the space)*. Look! There's a drop cloth.

MOSS. Maybe the body's under there. *(He goes to the drop cloth and ceremoniously lifts it. SERENA covers her eyes.)*

SERENA. Is it under there?

MOSS. Yeah. I knew we'd find it. There's maggots all in his eyes, and crawlin' out of his mouth.

SERENA. Oh, my God!

MOSS. Come have a look.

JESSIE. Ooooo. That's the worst thing I've ever seen. You gotta see this. *(She takes SERENA's shoulder to move her to the drop cloth. SERENA flinches.)*

SERENA. Don't touch me. I don't want to see it.

JESSIE. Let's put her under there with him.

MOSS. Yeah. Deadly.

JESSIE. You and Corky can hook up.

(They pick SERENA up but she kicks and screams.)

SERENA. No! No! Don't.

JESSIE *(holding up the drop cloth)*. Corky's not under there. It's a joke, Princess. Just a joke. God, you're so serious.

SERENA. I'm sorry. I thought it was really Corky. Dead. That's not funny.

JESSIE. Yes, it is. I hope we find him dead.

MOSS (*rummaging around the drop cloth*). Hey, look, there's a big blood stain on it.

JESSIE. Let me see that. Yeah. Blood.

SERENA. Ha! Now the joke's on you. Here's where your stain came from. Red paint. (*She holds up a can of red paint.*)

MOSS. That's not a paint stain. It's not the same color.

SERENA. It's red, isn't it?

MOSS. Paint dries darker. Everyone knows that.

JESSIE. I think it's blood. Corky's blood. Paint would flake off. This won't come off.

MOSS. It's blood awright.

JESSIE. Let's find the body.

SERENA (*shining her flashlight around*). Look at all the photos.

JESSIE. God! They're all Corky. Here's his middle school graduation. (*Laughing.*) He looks like a jerk.

MOSS. Who's that woman?

JESSIE. Don't know. Says "Maggie" on the back.

SERENA. Hey. That's old man Leisner with her. Only he's young.

JESSIE. Must be Corky's mom.

MOSS. Corky didn't have a mom.

JESSIE. He did once, didn't he? What was he, hatched?

MOSS. Well, what happened to her then?

JESSIE. Probably got sick of living with that old crazy man.

MOSS. Hey, what's this? (*His sudden movement jars a framed photo. It falls to the floor and breaks.*)

JESSIE. Look what you done.

MOSS. I didn't mean to do it. It's dark in here. I can't see.

SERENA. Be careful of the glass.

JESSIE. Just stand there and you won't get into any more trouble.

SERENA *(putting down her flashlight)*. Oh, my God.

JESSIE. What?

SERENA. Look here. It's clothes. A whole bag.

JESSIE. Let's see. *(She peers at the clothes and holds up a jacket.)* Oh, my God, I recognize this. It was Corky's.

SERENA. That's disgusting. A dead person's clothes.

JESSIE. Ugly, isn't it? I hate that color.

MOSS. He always wore this. Brian thought it was cool. The body must be here.

SERENA. Why would the old man keep his dead son's clothes?

JESSIE. Maybe he had 'em packed up to give to the poor.

SERENA. No. It's a shrine. To his dead son.

JESSIE. He worships it.

MOSS. Maybe he dresses and undresses the body like a doll.

JESSIE. Undressing a dead body? That's sick!

SERENA. Like that movie where the son dresses up like his mother.

MOSS *(zombielike)*. You wanna stay at my motel? You'll like it here. *(He leaps out at the girls making a huge noise. They scream. MOSS laughs hysterically.)*

JESSIE. You dumbass! You scared us half to death.

MOSS. What a joke. The two of you looked like you'd seen a ghost.

(SERENA's breathing is audible. She is very frightened and on the verge of tears. JESSIE shines her flashlight on SERENA.)

JESSIE. Serena. You all right?

(SERENA pushes MOSS, catching him off guard; he falls down.)

MOSS. Hey! It was a joke. That's all.
SERENA. Don't ever do that again!
JESSIE. Better watch out, Moss, she'll hurt you!
MOSS. You didn't have to push me.
JESSIE. She's a big scaredy-cat.
MOSS. She shouldn't have come with us.
SERENA. You made me. I'm lighting the candles.
JESSIE. Good idea. And, Moss, you stay where I can keep my eye on you.
MOSS. I'm right here.

(SERENA sets candles around the space. MOSS takes out his knife and plays with it.)

SERENA. Anybody got a light?
JESSIE *(taking out cigarette lighter)*. Here. I'll light one.
SERENA. Look at this. Here's something printed on school stationery.
MOSS. Probably a report on Corky cutting class.
SERENA. I can't see too well but it looks like a thank-you note. *(She tries to read by candlelight.)* Oh God, it's from Miss Asaro.
JESSIE. That old buzzard. What's it say?

SERENA. I can hardly read it. *(She reads.)* "Dear Mr. Leisner. Thank you for your visit to school and for returning my bracelet." *(They react with disdain.)* "The jewelry itself has little value, but the bracelet means a great deal to me as it belonged to my mother."

(MOSS snickers.)

JESSIE. She had a mother?

SERENA *(reading)*. "As you say, I'm sure Corky meant to return it."

JESSIE. That's a laugh. I'm sure Corky meant to steal it.

SERENA *(still reading)*. "It was a pleasure to finally see you at school. Sincerely, Miss Asaro."

MOSS. I remember that. Old Man Leisner came clankin' into school in the middle of the day.

JESSIE. God. I'd have died.

MOSS. I never saw Corky so pissed. Everyone laughing at him. He went and hid in the locker room. Brian dragged him out kicking and cursing. They ragged on him for weeks about that.

JESSIE. Serves him right for havin' an old man like that.

SERENA. He can't help who his dad is. No one can help that.

JESSIE. Look. Here's some more letters. Look at the fancy stationery. Pink!

SERENA. They're all the same. So many.

JESSIE. Read them to us.

SERENA. Me?

JESSIE. Yeah, you.

SERENA. I don't know if I should.

JESSIE. They might be clues. Go on. Read them.

SERENA. Here. Hold this.

(SERENA gives her flashlight to MOSS. During the following, JESSIE motions to MOSS behind SERENA's back, then whispers to him. MOSS backs away with the flashlight and the two hide quietly in the darkness.)

SERENA. "Dear Corky, I think about you every day and wait for the mail to come, hoping there'll be a letter from you. I know you can never forgive me, but someday maybe you'll understand why I couldn't stay." Jessie, I don't feel right reading these. They're too personal. Jessie? Where are you? Moss? *(There is utter silence.)* Jessie? Jessie!! Don't do this. It's not funny. Come back. Jessie. *(Pause.)* Okay. I can play this game. I'll just ignore you. *(She waits.)* I hate you both. I'll never do anything with you again. *(Pause.)* Jessie! *(She is crying now.)* Jessie, please. Moss! I'm scared. I told you I don't like to be scared. *(From the darkness MOSS makes an eerie sound.)* Come on, you two. This isn't funny. Oh, God. Don't. Please. Don't. *(The sound comes again. SERENA gropes around near her and grabs a wrench. Near hysteria.)* Stop it. Please. I'm so scared. Stop it. Please. Sweet Jesus, Mary and Joseph. Please. Please. Please. *(The sound of approaching footsteps from the street.)* Oh, my God. Help me.
JESSIE *(furiously)*. Ssshhhh.
MOSS. Shut up!
SERENA. Moss? Is that you?
MOSS. It's Leisner! Hide!
SERENA. Moss, where are you?
JESSIE. Shut up!

(Footsteps coming down the stairs. The door opens and LEISNER enters, tools clanking. He puts down his toolbox, takes off his jacket. He tries to switch on the light. No light. He switches the light several times. Still no light. He moves around in the darkness. There is the sound of something else moving in the dark.)

LEISNER. Who's there? Corky? Is that you? *(Silence. He steps on the broken picture frame. He kneels and sees the broken picture.)* Who's there? Come out. *(Silence. He sees the hacksaw misplaced. The pink stationery on the floor. Yelling:)* Come out! Out! Stupid kids. Messin' with my stuff. What gives you the right? I told you not to break in here again. I told you! *(Silence. He searches for the intruder.)* Where are you? Come out! *(He goes to the phone.)* I'll call the cops, that's what. They'll lock you up and throw away the key. No. The cops don't care. They don't care. I'll teach you a lesson you'll never forget. I'll teach you myself. *(He closes the door and locks it. Drops the key in his toolbag.)* Where are you? Where are you hidin'? I'll get you, you hear! *(He fumbles about in the dark, knocking things over. He moves directly to where SERENA is cowering in the dark. We hear her intake of breath.)* Gotcha!
SERENA *(screaming)*. Let go!
LEISNER. No!

(JESSIE runs forward to help SERENA. LEISNER grabs the wrench. There is a struggle. The thud of someone being hit. LEISNER gasps and falls. For a moment we hear his labored breathing. Then silence.)

MOSS. Jessie? Serena?

(MOSS turns his flashlight on LEISNER lying on the ground, blood seeping from a head wound. SERENA leans over him, holding a bloody wrench. JESSIE stands next to SERENA. SERENA screams and drops the wrench.)

MOSS. God! Look at the blood.
SERENA *(sobbing)*. You killed him.
JESSIE. Me? You hit him. I didn't do nothin'.
SERENA. He's dead! He's dead. Oh, my God, you killed him.
JESSIE. Shut up!
MOSS. What'd you belt him for?
JESSIE. I told you, it was her.
SERENA. You killed him. You killed him.
JESSIE. Liar! Moss, I didn't hit nobody. She did it. You saw her. She was holding the wrench, wasn't she?
SERENA. You killed him!

(JESSIE grabs SERENA and shakes her. SERENA is crying and sobbing.)

JESSIE. Shut up! Shut up!
MOSS. Stop it, both of you.
JESSIE. I didn't hit nobody. It was her.
MOSS. I believe you. Just shut up, so we can think what to do.
JESSIE. We got to get out of here. That's what.
MOSS. What about him?
JESSIE. Forget about him. We got to save ourselves.

SERENA. What if he isn't dead?

JESSIE. He's dead all right. Look at his head.

SERENA. We can't just leave him.

JESSIE. I can. Here help me get this window open. (*MOSS hesitates.*) I said, help me.

MOSS. We're in big trouble, Jess.

JESSIE. So check his pulse. See if he's breathin'.

MOSS. I'm not touchin' him.

JESSIE. Then shut up and help me get this window open. We got to get out of here.

SERENA (*bending down over LEISNER*). I think he's alive.

JESSIE. Who cares.

MOSS. We'll call the cops, then get out before they get here.

SERENA. No. We can't do that.

JESSIE. Well, finally, she makes some sense.

SERENA. If my dad finds out I was here...

JESSIE. That'd ruin your image, eh, Princess? No one's going to find out we were here because we're not calling the cops. (*She tries to open the window.*)

MOSS. You think you're so smart, don't you. Always bossin' everyone around. Well, there's something you didn't think of. And it's important.

JESSIE. Yeah, what?

MOSS. You're so smart, you figure it out.

JESSIE. I can't get this window open. It's jammed.

MOSS. If Old Man Leisner dies then you're a murderer!

JESSIE. Shut up! First of all, I didn't do it. She did. Second of all, I'm gettin' out of here, and third of all, if you ever say that again, I'll do to you what she did to him! Now get over here and help me with this window!

MOSS *(trying to open window)*. It's stuck tight. I can't budge it.

JESSIE. Here. I'll help you. *(They both try to open the window. It opens.)* Come on. Let's get out of here. *(JESSIE begins to climb out the window, then ducks back in.)* Jesus. There's people out there. *(JESSIE and MOSS flatten themselves against the wall. JESSIE closes the window.)* We've got to go out the same way we came in. *(JESSIE stands on the furniture but cannot reach the skylight.)*

MOSS. Jump!

JESSIE. I can't reach it, dumbass. Here. Lift me up.

MOSS. No. You'll go off and leave us here.

JESSIE. No, I won't. I'll go for help. I'll get Brian.

MOSS. I don't trust you.

JESSIE. I swore an oath, didn't I?

MOSS. Let Serena go. I'll lift her up.

JESSIE. That's a stupid idea.

MOSS. Why? Because it's not you goin'?

JESSIE. That's right. Now lift me up. *(MOSS climbs on the furniture with JESSIE. He lifts her up toward the skylight.)* Higher. I can't reach it. *(MOSS lifts JESSIE higher.)* Higher. *(MOSS lifts JESSIE as high as he can. He loses his balance and the two fall.)* Shit!

MOSS. Ow. My leg. I hurt myself.

JESSIE. Shut up, you big baby. You're not hurt.

MOSS. Yes I am. I hit my leg on that ledge.

SERENA. Let me see. Right there?

MOSS. Ow. Oh. I'm not sure I can walk.

JESSIE. You can walk. *(She prowls the space.)* Wait. Stupid. We'll go out the door.

SERENA. Into the street? What if someone sees us? I'd rather die than get caught.

JESSIE. I'm not gonna die or get caught. We'll make sure no one's out there, then make a run for it one at a time.

SERENA. Just because you can't see anyone doesn't mean someone isn't watching.

MOSS. That's true. I'm with Serena. It's too risky.

JESSIE. Well, I'm not goin' to prison for this old pervert!

MOSS (*limping to the phone*). I'm callin' Brian. He'll get us out of this.

JESSIE. No. If you call Brian they can trace the call to your house.

MOSS. So what?

JESSIE. So what? It'll prove you were here, genius.

SERENA. I saw that on TV. That's how they caught that serial killer.

(*MOSS takes out his knife and begins playing with it.*)

JESSIE. That's right. We're not using the phone, so forget it. Put that thing away.

MOSS. Make me.

(*JESSIE lunges for MOSS. The sound of a police siren coming from the street.*)

SERENA. Oh, my God. They're comin'.

(*Pandemonium. SERENA cowers. MOSS and JESSIE go for the door and both struggle to open it.*)

MOSS. Get out of the way, you. Move!

(MOSS pushes JESSIE out of the way and she falls. The police siren peaks, then fades. SERENA is sobbing with relief.)

SERENA. It wasn't for us. They weren't coming here.

JESSIE *(laughing)*. Probably going to your house for Brian!

MOSS. Ha. Ha. Think you're so funny. The door won't open. Old Man Leisner locked it.

JESSIE. Here. Let me try. *(She struggles with the door. It is locked tight.)* Jesus. We stepped in it now.

MOSS. What are we gonna do?

JESSIE. Maybe the key's in his pocket. *(Pause.)* One of us has to search him.

MOSS. Not me.

JESSIE. You're useless, you know that?

SERENA. I'll look.

JESSIE. Hey, Princess. At least somebody around here has some guts.

MOSS. Shut up. I don't see you touchin' him.

(SERENA carefully feels in LEISNER's pockets.)

JESSIE. Check his shirt.

SERENA. I can't find it.

JESSIE. Where did he put it?

SERENA. It's not here.

MOSS. Look in his back pockets.

SERENA *(starting to roll him over, then stopping)*. I think he's dead. I feel sick.

JESSIE. Get out of the way. *(She searches in LEISNER's back pockets.)* Nothing there.

MOSS. Maybe he dropped it.

JESSIE. It could be anywhere. There must be another way out.

(All three look around for another possible exit. LEIS-NER shifts position on the floor. The others don't see.)

MOSS. I say we go out the window.

SERENA. The window's no good. Someone'll see us for sure.

JESSIE. I don't care. I'm not spending the night with a dead body.

MOSS. The window's all we got.

JESSIE. Don't be stupid. We have to think this through.

MOSS. I've thought it through. I want out of here.

JESSIE. You never thought anything through in your life. We have to get our stories straight.

MOSS. What do you mean, our stories?

JESSIE. Well, if we get caught they're going to question us, aren't they?

SERENA. Like they questioned Old Man Leisner about Corky.

JESSIE. So, if we tell different stories, they'll know we're lying, at least some of us are lying.

MOSS. Jesus. I didn't do nothin'. I just wanted to trash Old Man Leisner's place.

SERENA. I didn't want to come at all. You made me.

JESSIE. What did we do? Tie you up and drag you? Hold a gun to your head? Nobody made you, Princess.

SERENA. You said I had to be initiated.

JESSIE. So? You made the choice, didn't you? What a baby. Tryin' to blame everyone else.

MOSS. Blaming's chicken.

JESSIE. So you're the brave one?

MOSS. I'm Brian's brother, ain't I?

JESSIE. Well, then, you're willing to take your share of the blame.

MOSS. Blame? I didn't do nothin'.

JESSIE. So you're blamin' this whole mess on me?

MOSS. It wasn't me who slammed the old man, was it!

JESSIE. If I told you once I told you a thousand times. She did it! It was her!

SERENA. I didn't do it! She's lying.

JESSIE. Here's the way it goes. If we get caught, we say it was her.

SERENA. No!

JESSIE. Two against one.

SERENA. But I didn't do it! I was scared, but I would never hit someone.

JESSIE. You think Moss's going to believe you, candy-ass kiss-up!

SERENA. Leave me alone.

JESSIE. Leave you alone? That's all you care about, right? The rest of us can go to hell for all you care. Right?

SERENA. Please. Leave me alone.

JESSIE. 'Cause we're just a bunch of losers to you. (She imitates SERENA whining.) Please don't tell I was here. I can't get caught. Daddy'll be angry at his little girl.

SERENA. Stop it!

JESSIE. Mommy and Daddy might find out you're not their perfect AP class daughter! Well, Miss Head Stuck Up Your Ass, you'll just have to take it with the rest of us.

MOSS. That's enough, Jess. Leave her alone.

JESSIE. You can have her when I'm done with her. And I'm not done yet.

SERENA. You don't understand.

JESSIE. I understand all right. We're not taking the blame for what you did! Do you hear me! You did it! And when they ask us, we'll tell them it was you!

SERENA. Shut up! Shut up!

JESSIE. And they'll lock you up and throw away the key!

SERENA. No! No! No!

MOSS. Stop it! Leave her alone!

SERENA. Look. Look at me. See that? See it?

(SERENA pulls her shirt down to reveal her back. Large welts and bruises crisscross her entire back. JESSIE stares but MOSS turns away.)

JESSIE. Jesus.

SERENA. Look at me. Now do you see why I can't get caught? What do you think'll happen to me if I get caught? Look at me!

MOSS. Who did this to you?

JESSIE. Who do you think? Dear old Dad, I bet.

SERENA. He says it's the only way I'll learn.

MOSS. Learn what?

SERENA. I don't know. Everything. Nothing. I don't know.

JESSIE. You must have done something awful bad.

SERENA. I guess so. I don't know.

MOSS. You mean you don't know what you did?

SERENA. I try to be good. I try.

MOSS. You must have done something.

JESSIE. Shut up, Moss. She didn't do nothin'. You didn't do nothin'. Here. Get dressed.

(JESSIE helps SERENA pull her shirt back on. MOSS plays with his knife.)

MOSS. I oughta give your old man a taste of his own medicine.

JESSIE. Put that thing away.

MOSS. Make me. *(JESSIE goes to MOSS and takes his knife.)* Hey. Give my knife back. You can't just take it.

JESSIE. We got to get our story straight. Then I'll give you back your stupid knife.

MOSS. This again.

JESSIE. We got to agree on one story to tell so that we protect each other. We swore, remember?

SERENA. How are you going to protect me?

JESSIE. I don't know yet, but I'm thinkin'.

MOSS. Hurry up. I'm freakin' out here.

(LEISNER moves. They don't see.)

JESSIE. I say we go out the street window one at a time. Maybe there's no one out there now. One of us can be lookout.

SERENA. I'm too scared.

JESSIE. Stay behind if you like. I'm goin'.

SERENA. I thought you were gonna protect me.

JESSIE. I can't help you if you won't help yourself. Give me that wrench.

(MOSS picks up the wrench.)

SERENA. Wait. What're you gonna do with that?

JESSIE. I'm gonna finish him off.

SERENA. What?

JESSIE. In case he's not dead. So he can't talk. Then there's only us.

MOSS. You're crazy.

JESSIE. It's not crazy to save yourself, is it?

SERENA. It's crazy to kill someone.

JESSIE. You listen to me. He's seen us. He knows. He'll tell the cops. Besides, he's dead already. I'm just makin' sure. It's not like anyone'll miss him.

MOSS. That's true.

SERENA. He's a person.

JESSIE. He's not a person, he's a freak, a pervert. He killed his son.

SERENA. But we don't know that. Not for sure.

MOSS. I'm getting out of here.

(JESSIE stops MOSS. They struggle for possession of the wrench.)

LEISNER. Corky! Sweet Jesus, Corky! Stop it!

(JESSIE and MOSS stop their struggle. MOSS turns his flashlight on LEISNER. LEISNER moves toward MOSS and JESSIE.)

MOSS. Get away.

LEISNER *(keeps coming)*. Corky! Corky!

MOSS. Get away from me!

(MOSS raises the wrench to defend himself. LEISNER flinches as though MOSS is going to hit him. LEISNER sees the wrench, tries to take it from MOSS. The two struggle, then MOSS forces LEISNER to his knees.)

JESSIE. Hit him! Finish him off!

LEISNER. Don't hit me, Corky. Don't hit me no more. I try to be good. I try.

(JESSIE grabs the wrench and moves to strike LEISNER. SERENA blocks her path.)

SERENA. No, don't hit him.

(MOSS takes the wrench from JESSIE.)

LEISNER *(babbling)*. Don't hit me no more, Corky. I won't call the cops. I never called the cops. I'll be good. Don't hit me.

MOSS *(realizing, drops the wrench)*. Sweet Jesus.

SERENA. There. It's all right. He won't hit you.

LEISNER. Maggie? Dear God in heaven, Maggie.

SERENA. I'm not Maggie, Mr. Leisner.

LEISNER *(reaching out to SERENA)*. Tell Corky not to hit me.

SERENA. I'll tell him. I'll tell him.

LEISNER *(clinging to SERENA)*. Thank God you're here. He tried to kill me, Maggie. Don't let him hurt me again.

SERENA. I won't let him hurt you.

LEISNER. I'm sorry, Corky. I'm sorry. Don't hit me anymore.

MOSS. I'm not Corky, Mr. Leisner.

LEISNER. I'm sorry, Corky. I'm sorry.

JESSIE *(taking the wrench and standing over LEISNER)*. Well, this is a touching moment. But I'm not going to prison. Give me the key, old man. *(LEISNER does not respond. JESSIE grabs him and shakes him.)* Give me the key to that door.

LEISNER. I give it to Corky.

SERENA. He doesn't understand.

JESSIE. He'll understand this. *(She drops the wrench and takes out MOSS's knife.)* Give me the key!

LEISNER *(cowering)*. Don't. Please.

JESSIE. Give me that key. Now! *(She goes for LEISNER.)*

SERENA. No! I won't let you hurt him!

(SERENA protects LEISNER. The two girls struggle.)

MOSS. Stop it! Leave her alone!

(MOSS defends SERENA. JESSIE stabs MOSS. He staggers and falls. JESSIE drops the knife.)

SERENA. Oh, my God! Moss!

MOSS. Look what you done. Look what you gone and done. You cut me.

JESSIE. I didn't mean to. It was self-defense. She attacked me.

SERENA. I didn't. You know I didn't.

MOSS. You stabbed me. I'm bleedin'.

JESSIE. It was your fault. You should've stayed out of it. It was between me and her!

MOSS. Jesus. I'm hurt.

SERENA. Oh, my God.

JESSIE. If we don't get out of here, we're done for. *(To LEISNER.)* Give me that key.

SERENA. Give her the key, Mr. Leisner.

LEISNER *(pointing to the toolbag by the door)*. Over there. In the bag.

(JESSIE rummages in the toolbag, finds the key and unlocks the door.)

JESSIE. I'm getting out of here. You can go straight to hell for all I care!

MOSS. It was you, wasn't it? You slammed Old Man Leisner.

JESSIE. So what if I did? You can't prove it. Nobody'll believe that old crazy man. Serena here's too scared to tell. And you'd never rat me out, Moss, would you? *(Silence.)* That stupid fish was right. You are a dead one. *(She exits.)*

MOSS. Jessie! Wait! Help me! *(He crawls toward the door and looks out, then falls.)*

SERENA. You're bleeding. Please. Let me get some help.

MOSS. No. I gotta get out of here.

SERENA. Then I'll go with you.

MOSS. No. You can't get in trouble. I don't want you to get in trouble.

SERENA. I don't care anymore.

LEISNER. Don't leave me, Maggie.

MOSS. Don't follow me. Let me go. I won't tell about you, Serena. I won't. No matter what. *(He stumbles through the door and exits.)*

LEISNER. Corky? Corky?

SERENA. He's gone, Mr. Leisner.

LEISNER. But he'll come back. He always comes back.

SERENA. He hurt you, didn't he?

LEISNER. He hurt me. He's always hurting me.

SERENA. I know. I know. I'm sorry. I'm so sorry, Mr. Leisner, for what I thought about you, for breaking in, everything. I just keep messing up. I try to do what's right but I keep doing everything wrong. It's all my fault.

LEISNER. That's not true. You're a brave girl. A good girl. You protected me.

SERENA. I guess I did.

LEISNER. Shhh, Maggie, shhhh. It's all right now. You're home.

SERENA. I'm not Maggie, Mr. Leisner.

LEISNER. You're not?

SERENA. No, I'm Serena.

LEISNER. Serena. That's a lovely name. Don't leave me, Serena.

SERENA. I won't. I won't let Corky hurt you again. No more hurting. Ever.

(The two hold each other as the lights fade.)

(Lights shift. Metal sound effects surge then diminish as JESSIE enters and shines her flashlight on the audience.)

JESSIE. You know, you can't trust anybody. I know that for sure now. Every time you give somebody a chance to do the smart thing they screw up. Like Moss. What a dumbass. If he'd just listened to me it would have been all right. But no, he had to get in the middle of it. It turned out okay though. They never suspected me. Gang

related, they called it. Front page of all the papers. I
went to the funeral. Ma wanted me to go with her, but I
went with Brian. We're hooked up now. I got him
wrapped around my little finger. Serena? Turned out she
didn't have it so good as we thought. Her and her mom,
they moved out of the house. They're livin' on my block
now. Guess she'll be all right. I got an eye on her.
(Pause.) Listen to me. You have to look out for yourself
in this world. 'Cause nobody's gonna do it for you. You
have to be smart. Not like with books and all that, but
smart in the world. Knowin' what to expect. Knowin'
what people will do to you. And then do it to them first.
I'm smart like that. I know how to take care of myself.
Now that Brian and me are hooked up I got nothin' to
worry about. No one touches me. I'm the one they listen
to. Moss and me finally did something big.

*(Metal sound effects surge and diminish as SERENA en-
ters.)*

SERENA. Jessie was right about me. I was too scared to
tell. I just didn't answer when they asked their questions.
Like I was in shock. I don't know. Maybe I was. I
showed that policewoman my back. She was so nice.
She called my mom and told us what we had to do. I
won't see my dad for a while now. He calls, but me and
my mom don't really want to talk to him. This morning
I looked out my bedroom window and Mr. Leisner was
there. Standing on the street. When he saw me he put
down his tools, opened a can of paint and began to paint
the house. Mom came out and they had this long conversation. Then she came up to my room and told me that it

was his way of saying thank you for what I had done for him. I cried then for the first time since that night. I can't stop thinking about Moss. I feel bad I never really got the chance to know him. It would never have happened if Moss hadn't tried to protect me, just like he promised. I got your back, he swore and I swore it, too. I keep thinking about how he risked everything for me. And Jessie. How she got away with it, just like Corky. So I have to tell. For Moss. I have to stand up for him the way he stood up for me. It's my way of saying thank you just like Mr. Leisner. I'm not sure what will happen. All I know is this is what I have to do, what I want to do. I think maybe that's what that fish was trying to say...about independence.

(*Sound effects surge and diminish as SERENA and JESSIE shine their flashlights on the empty spot where MOSS gave his monologue in the first scene. Silence. Lights fade to blackout.*)

END OF PLAY

Post Performance Forum
Designed and written by Laurie Brooks

Following the final blackout, the audience is greeted by the facilitators, who introduce themselves and invite the audience to participate in a brief post-performance experience. The Forum can be as long as an hour or as short as twenty minutes. The facilitators take the audience through five steps that encourage them to travel deeper into the actions and emotions of the characters in the play, providing an opportunity for the audience to express their views about the characters' choices and the consequences of their actions. For the Forum premiere, the actors playing Jessie and Serena functioned together as facilitators, but one facilitator may be used.

The Forum will require a statement from the D.A.'s office on how Jessie and Serena might be prosecuted and punished according to current laws in your state. Handheld microphones are recommended for the facilitators.

Printing related hotline telephone numbers in the program is suggested.

Part 1. Agree and Disagree Statements

Facilitators read the series of agree and disagree statements. As each statement is read, audience members stand in support if they agree and remain seated in protest if they disagree. This all-group opening exercise provides a safe environment for the expression of audience opinions and strong visual images regarding character actions in the play.

Statements

1. Serena was an innocent victim. None of this was her fault.
2. Jessie, Moss and Serena are equally responsible for what happened.
3. If you swear an oath you should never break it, no matter what.
4. Violence causes violence.
5. Moss deserved what he got at the end.
6. Brian would have been proud of his little brother, Moss.
7. When push comes to shove, most people care more about themselves than their friends.
8. What happened to Jessie, Moss and Serena could happen to any one of you.

Part 2. Crimes and Punishments

Facilitators call on a representative from the D.A.'s office or other law enforcement officer to read the statement on how Serena and Jessie might be *charged* and how they might be *punished* according to current laws in your state. Now the audience becomes aware of and can reflect on the consequences of the characters' choices. Acknowledge other professional representatives in the audience and mention availability of literature after the Forum.

Part 3. Counselors

Facilitators suggest that Serena and Jessie have not only broken laws, they also hurt each other and themselves. Putting the audience members into role as counselors, they are asked to stand, sharing wrongs Jessie and Serena committed against their friends or themselves. Facilitators ask participants to brainstorm ideas on the multiple factors that contributed to the choices made by Serena and Jessie in the play, encouraging the use of "I" messages. Through taking on the role of counselors, audience members are empowered to identify hurtful behavior and the factors that may have caused it.

Part 4. Moss Speaks

Facilitators remind students that one character won't have an opportunity to change or learn from what happened.

Facilitators ask the audience what Moss might say about what happened if he could speak to us now. What would Moss say to Jessie and Serena?

Facilitators acknowledge several responses. Moss appears in silhouette and responds.

Part 5. Closure

Students are asked to stand popcorn-style and offer a phrase or brief sentence that might be offered at Moss' memorial service. As they exit the theatre, audience members are encouraged to leave further thoughts for the characters on outlines of Jessie, Moss and Serena that create a graffiti wall in the lobby or outside the theatre.

Forum Dialogue

The following sample dialogue is intended to assist with the smooth execution of the Forum. Some adjustment is to be expected, according to the personalities of the facilitators and the circumstances surrounding each Forum as it unfolds. A memorized-sounding version is to be avoided. There must be a sense of individuality each time, played in the moment, according to the responses of the audience. It is wise to rehearse the Forum with test audiences, to give the facilitators as much practice as possible. Ongoing monitoring of the Forum is suggested, thinking of it as in continual development, with notes given to facilitators throughout a run.

Introduction

Facilitator 1: "Good evening. My name is _____ (name of facilitator). I'm an actor and I played _____ (character name) in *Deadly Weapons*."

Facilitator 2: "And my name is _____. I'm also an actor and I played _____. We'd like to ask you to join us in an exploration of the characters and their actions in *Deadly Weapons*. We want to hear what you think about what happened to these characters, especially Serena and Jessie. But before we begin we need to agree on some basic rules. There'll be no name-calling of the characters or each other and no cursing or inappropriate language. Agreed?"

Wait for their response. If it's not enthusiastic enough...

Facilitator 1: "I didn't hear you. Can we agree on that? Good."

Part 1. Agree and Disagree Statements

Facilitator 2: "We're going to read a series of statements that relate to the play. If you agree with the statement, stand in support. If you disagree, remain seated in protest. Stand if you agree. Stay seated if you disagree. Ready?"

Facilitators take turns reading the statements, giving the audience time to stand or remain seated, asking them all to sit before continuing with the next statement. Facilitators avoid judging audience response to statements by saying "very good" or other positive or negative commentary as a result of strong agreement or disagreement. Rather, facilitators offer factual comments such as, "I see about half of you are standing in agreement." or simply say, "Thank you."

Part 2. Choices and Actions

Facilitator 1: "We're fortunate to have with us in the audience today a representative from _____ (your city or state) district attorney's office. I'd like to introduce _____ (name of representative). Will you share with us what charges Serena and Jessie might face in this state?"

Representative comes forward and reads prepared statement into the microphone.

Sample Prosecutor's Statement

"These charges and punishments have been determined after an initial conference on the actions of Jessie and Serena in the play. A full investigation and trial would be required to accurately determine the official charges and prosecution. _____ (your state's) law states that alleged offenders under the age of seventeen will be prosecuted as juveniles. However, Jessie might be tried as an adult. Here are the potential charges:

• Burglary of a habitation with an intent to commit Aggravated Assault. (Jessie and Serena broke into Leisner's house with a concealed weapon.)
• Aggravated Assault with a deadly weapon. (Jessie used a wrench to hit Leisner, resulting in serious injury.)
• Manslaughter. (In the struggle for possession of the knife, Jessie fatally stabs Moss. Jessie's purpose for obtaining the knife is to kill Leisner.)

The punishments for these crimes could include:
• 5 to 99 years in the penitentiary for burglary of a habitation with intent to commit aggravated assault.
• 2 to 20 years for aggravated assault with a deadly weapon.
• 2 to 20 years for manslaughter."

Facilitator 2: "Thank you. And thanks for joining us today. We want to let you know that this production also has the support of _____ (mentions agencies who have partnered with theatre). These agencies have generously provided us with literature that will be available for you in the lobby after the performance."

Facilitator 1: "So now we know something about how the state of _____ would view the actions of Serena and Jessie in the play. Now it's your turn. Jessie and Serena have broken laws but they are also guilty of hurting each other and themselves. We're going to ask you to take on the role of counselors to help Jessie and Serena target their mistakes."

Facilitator 2: "You know how sometimes it takes someone else to show you your mistakes? Well, that's what we're asking you to do for Jessie and Serena. Imagine that you are experts in counseling others, like peer educators. Say the name of the character first and then the wrong they have done against someone else or to themselves. Begin your comments with "I think" or "I feel.""

Facilitators offer examples, such as:

Facilitator 1: "Jessie bullied Serena into going into Leisner's house when she didn't really want to."

After each response, Facilitators thank the speaker and ask: "Who's next?" or "Who has another idea?"

Facilitator 2: "Great. Thanks for all those comments. We'd like to take this discussion a little deeper. What do you think are some of the factors that contributed to the choices that Serena and Jessie made in the play? Why did these two do what they did?"

Facilitators call on as many participants as time permits, thanking each respondent. If an audience member asks about Moss, suggest comments on Moss be held for a moment, that he will be discussed next.

Part 3. Moss Speaks

Facilitator 1: "Now there's one character who won't have an opportunity to change or learn or even think about what happened." (Audience response.)

Facilitator 2: "That's right. Moss. If he could talk to us now, what do you think Moss might say? What do you think he would say to Serena? How about Jessie?"

Facilitators acknowledge several responses from the audience, thanking each respondent.

Facilitator 1: "Let's listen to Moss."

Moss appears in silhouette and makes his statement.

Moss' Response

"I hope Serena's okay. I hope her dad will stop hurting her. I wish I could've helped her, taken care of her. I wanted to be her bodyguard. I should have stopped Jessie. I should have stopped all the hurting.

You swore, Jessie, but you're a liar. You would never take the fall for me. I got your back you said, but you only looked out for number one. You're the one who's stupid, I think, and two-faced. You cut me, then just ran away... I was your friend. Didn't that mean anything to you? I just wanted to have some fun. I wasn't supposed to die.

I know I made mistakes. But I never meant to hurt anyone. I'm sorry. I'm so awful sorry. I guess I got what I deserved. It was my own fault. After all, I brought the knife."

Moss fades and exits.

Facilitator 2: "Was that what you expected?"

Facilitators acknowledge several responses to their question.

Part 4: Closure

Facilitator 2: "Now we're going to ask you to imagine that we're at a memorial service for Moss. If you'd like, you can stand and offer a phrase or short sentence to remember Moss. It might be words of comfort or advice or it might be an epitaph that's written on his gravestone. Just stand when you're ready and take turns."

Facilitators are silent if possible during the response to create mood, allowing the audience to negotiate this part of the Forum.

Facilitator 1: "Thank you. I know that Moss would appreciate that."

Facilitator 2: "Thanks very much for participating in this discussion. We'd like to invite you to contribute messages to Serena, Jessie and Moss on our graffiti wall in the lobby with words, drawings and graffiti art. We want you to express yourselves, but please be respectful. Like in the classroom there'll be no name-calling and no curses and if you're tempted to write your phone number, be assured that no one will call. We also hope that you will continue the dialogue we have begun today with your friends, parents or professionals. And please...be good to yourselves and others. Thank you very much."

End Forum

Facilitating the Post-Performance Forum

Take charge.
Facilitation has been called the "velvet fist." Using few words, establish benevolent leadership, explaining each step with simple, clear directions. Never ask participants' permission by ending sentences with, "Okay?" Your clarity of purpose and leadership will help the audience's comfort level and encourage participation.

Make a safe space.
Always let the audience know that differing points of view are welcomed. Set clear rules of no name-calling and no cursing. Respect for each other is crucial to the success of the Forum.

Never make judgments or offer personal opinions.
A facilitator does not decide what is good and bad, right or wrong. A facilitator is accepting of all points of view.

Listen carefully.
A successful facilitator knows how to listen for what is said and what is not said. Due to the size of the space, it is wise to repeat what participants have said so that everyone is included. Paraphrase their remarks and then ask if you've repeated the gist of their ideas correctly.

Serve as a role model.
Facilitators must always address a prejudiced remark or misinformation. Never challenge the person directly. Rather, ask the group, "Would anyone like to respond to that thought?" or "Does everyone here agree with that

idea?" The facilitator remains neutral and the group is encouraged to offer their opinions.

Use "I" messages.
Encouraging the group to begin their comments by saying "I think..." or "I feel..." asks participants to own their individual opinions and avoids defensiveness and accusation.

Silence is effective.
Pauses in the Forum give participants time to think. Do not be in a hurry to move on too quickly. If no one is participating, it may be because they are unclear. Offer another example or rephrase the instructions. You may want to ask, "Does everyone understand what I'm asking you to do?"

Practice inclusion.
Keep your eyes moving, scanning the entire audience for those who wish to participate. Encourage the group without singling out individuals. If one person monopolizes the Forum, gently interrupt saying, "Thank you. I'm going to stop you there, so we can have time for everyone who wants to share."

Keep your sense of humor.
Laughter puts everyone at ease and encourages camaraderie between the audience and the facilitator.

Be human.
Never adopt a didactic attitude that says, "I'm the teacher. I know more than you do." Your job is to empower the participants through inviting them to share their opinions.

Practice conflict resolution.
If conflict occurs, freeze the moment by stopping the conversation. Then state clearly what you see happening. This distances the conflict from the people involved. Ask other participants to comment or move on.

Timing is crucial.
Remain as flexible as possible with time. Acknowledge at the opening of the Forum that time will be short. Look for appropriate moments to make transitions from one part of the Forum to another. Always give warnings, such as, "I'll take two more comments," or "Two more minutes, then we have to move on."

Encourage further discussion.
Always end the Forum by encouraging participants to continue exploring the ideas in the play with someone they trust—friends, family members or professionals.

DIRECTOR'S NOTES